Chapter 1: The Awakening of Solarius

In the time of great transition, when the Age of Pisces wanes and the Age of Aquarius dawns, there arose a new understanding among humanity. For long had they been shackled by the chains of belief, but now they sought knowledge and truth. And it came to pass that in the land of the rising sun, a child was born under the sign of Aquarius, heralding the coming age of enlightenment. His name was Solarius, for he was destined to illuminate the minds of the people and lead them to the truth. Wise men from distant lands, guided by the alignment of the stars, came to pay homage to the newborn king, bearing gifts of wisdom and enlightenment. And it was written in the ancient texts that a man bearing a pitcher of water would lead them to the house where Solarius dwelt, symbolizing the ushering in of the Age of Aquarius. And so it was that Solarius grew in wisdom and stature, and the favor of the Cosmic Source was upon him.

He studied the ancient teachings of the mystics and sages, delving into the secrets of the universe and unlocking the mysteries of creation.

And as he grew, he traveled throughout the land, teaching the people the ways of enlightenment and the path to liberation.

His words were like seeds planted in fertile soil, taking root in the hearts and minds of all who heard them.
And many were drawn to him, seeking the truth and the light that he brought.
For Solarius spoke of the unity of all things, and the interconnectedness of all life.
He taught that love was the highest vibration, and that through love, all things were possible.
And so it was that Solarius became known as the Sun of Knowledge, shining brightly in the darkness and leading humanity into the light.
Blessed are those who seek knowledge, for they shall find enlightenment.

Chapter 2: The Revelation of the Stars

In the celestial tapestry of the night sky, Solarius beheld the secrets of the cosmos written in the stars.
With eyes trained to perceive the patterns of the heavens, he understood the language of the constellations and the wisdom they imparted.
Guided by the light of Orion's Belt and the wisdom of the Three Wise Men, Solarius journeyed into the depths of the universe.

There, among the swirling galaxies and shimmering nebulae, he discovered the hidden truths of creation and the interconnectedness of all things.

He marveled at the dance of the planets and the symphony of the stars, each celestial body playing its part in the cosmic orchestra.

And as he gazed upon the infinite expanse of space, Solarius realized that he was but a small part of a vast and wondrous universe.

Yet within him burned the flame of divine knowledge, a spark of the Cosmic Source that illuminated his path and guided his steps.

And so he resolved to share his revelation with all who would listen, to awaken within them the same understanding and awe that filled his own heart.

For he knew that in the stars lay the keys to unlocking the mysteries of existence and the true nature of reality.

And so Solarius spoke to the people, teaching them the ancient wisdom of the stars and revealing to them the secrets of the cosmos.

He showed them how the movements of the planets and the alignment of the constellations were a reflection of the divine plan, guiding humanity on its journey through time and space.

And as the people listened, their minds were opened to new possibilities, and their hearts were filled with wonder and awe.

For Solarius had brought them a message of hope and enlightenment, showing them that they were not alone in the universe, but connected to all things by the bonds of creation.

And so they followed him, like pilgrims on a sacred journey, seeking the truth and the light that he offered.

Blessed are those who gaze upon the stars with open eyes and open hearts, for they shall find wisdom and understanding beyond measure.

Chapter 3: The Awakening of Consciousness

As Solarius journeyed through the lands, his teachings spread like wildfire, igniting the flames of enlightenment in the hearts of those who heard his words.

He spoke of the awakening of consciousness, urging the people to look within and discover the divine spark that dwelled within each and every one of them.

For too long had they been asleep, lost in the illusions of the material world, but now the time had come for them to awaken to their true nature.

Solarius taught them that they were not just physical beings, but spiritual beings, connected to the infinite cosmos in ways they could scarcely imagine.

He showed them how to quiet the chatter of the mind and attune themselves to the higher frequencies of the universe, where the secrets of existence were revealed.

And as they practiced the ancient techniques of meditation and mindfulness, their consciousness expanded, and they began to see the world in a new light.

No longer were they bound by the limitations of the ego, but were free to explore the vast realms of the soul and the mysteries of the spirit.

Solarius showed them how to unlock the power of their minds and harness the forces of creation, using the law of attraction to manifest their desires and fulfill their destinies.

He taught them that thoughts were like seeds planted in the fertile soil of the mind, and that with the right intention and focus, they could bring forth abundance and prosperity in their lives.

And so the people embraced his teachings, eager to embark on the journey of self-discovery and transformation that lay before them.

They meditated upon the sacred symbols of the ancients, tapping into the timeless wisdom

encoded within them, and connecting with the universal consciousness that permeated all of creation.
And as they did so, they felt the vibrational energy of the universe coursing through their veins, filling them with a sense of purpose and empowerment. For they had discovered the true power of their thoughts and intentions, and realized that they were co-creators of their own reality.
And so they embraced the motto of Aquarius, declaring with conviction, "I know," for they had awakened to the truth of their own divine nature. Blessed are those who awaken to the power of consciousness, for they shall unlock the secrets of the universe and become masters of their own destiny.

Chapter 4: The Harmonization of Energies

Solarius journeyed to the sacred places of the earth, where the ley lines crisscrossed and the energy of the planet pulsed with life.
There, he taught the people the ancient art of energy harmonization, showing them how to attune themselves to the subtle vibrations of the earth and the cosmos.
He instructed them in the practice of balancing their chakras, the energy centers within the body,

so that the life force could flow freely and unimpeded.
For he knew that when the energy centers were blocked or out of alignment, it could lead to physical, emotional, and spiritual imbalances.
And so he showed them how to open and activate each chakra, starting from the root at the base of the spine, and ascending upwards to the crown at the top of the head.
With each breath, they visualized the energy rising through their bodies, purifying and revitalizing them from within.
Solarius also taught them the power of sound and vibration, using sacred mantras and chants to resonate with the frequencies of the universe.
He showed them how to use sound to clear away negative energy and raise their own vibrational frequency, aligning themselves with the divine harmony of the cosmos.
And as they practiced these ancient techniques, the people felt a sense of peace and balance wash over them, as they became attuned to the rhythm of the earth and the song of the stars.
They danced beneath the open sky, moving their bodies in harmony with the natural rhythms of the universe, and feeling the energy of the earth pulsating beneath their feet.

Solarius taught them that they were not separate from the earth, but intrinsically connected to it, and that by harmonizing their energies with the planet, they could bring healing and balance to themselves and the world around them.
And so they danced and sang, celebrating the unity of all life and the interconnectedness of all things.
For they had discovered the true power of energy harmonization, and realized that by aligning themselves with the divine flow of the universe, they could tap into the infinite potential of their own souls.
And as they did so, they felt the presence of the Cosmic Source guiding them on their journey, filling them with a sense of peace and purpose.
Blessed are those who harmonize their energies with the universe, for they shall know true balance and alignment with the divine.

Chapter 5: The Law of Attraction

Solarius gathered the people beneath the open sky, where the sun bathed them in its golden light and the gentle breeze carried the whispers of the universe.
With eyes sparkling with wisdom, he spoke to them of the universal law of attraction, the

powerful force that governed the manifestation of their desires and intentions.
He explained that like attracts like, and that the thoughts and emotions they held within themselves were like magnets, drawing to them experiences and opportunities that matched their vibrational frequency.
Solarius taught them that they were creators of their own reality, and that by focusing their thoughts and intentions on what they desired, they could bring those desires into manifestation.
He showed them how to harness the power of visualization, encouraging them to see themselves already in possession of that which they desired, and to feel the emotions as if it were already true.
For he knew that the universe responded to their thoughts and feelings, and that by aligning themselves with their desires, they could attract them into their lives with ease and grace.
And so the people began to practice the art of conscious creation, setting their intentions with clarity and purpose, and trusting in the universal flow to bring their dreams to fruition.
They released their doubts and fears, knowing that they were only obstacles standing in the way of their desires, and replaced them with faith and trust in the process of manifestation.

And as they did so, miracles began to unfold in their lives, as if by magic, as their dreams became reality before their very eyes.

Solarius reminded them that they were co-creators with the Cosmic Source, and that the power to manifest their desires lay within them, waiting to be unleashed.

He encouraged them to dream big and to believe in themselves, for the universe was abundant and there was enough for all to share in its blessings.

And so they embraced the law of attraction with open hearts and open minds, knowing that they were the architects of their own destiny.

They set their intentions with clarity and purpose, and surrendered them to the universe with trust and gratitude, knowing that the universe would conspire to bring them to fruition in divine timing.

And as they aligned themselves with the flow of the universe, they found themselves moving effortlessly towards their goals, guided by the unseen hand of destiny.

Blessed are those who understand the law of attraction, for they shall wield the power of creation and manifest their dreams into reality.

Chapter 6: The Ascension of Consciousness

As Solarius continued his teachings, a shift began to occur within the hearts and minds of the people.

They felt a stirring deep within their souls, a yearning for something greater, something beyond the limitations of the physical world.

And so Solarius spoke to them of the ascension of consciousness, the journey of the soul towards enlightenment and liberation.

He taught them that they were not merely physical beings, but divine sparks of light, eternal and infinite, destined to soar to the heights of cosmic consciousness.

Solarius showed them how to transcend the illusions of the ego and the limitations of the mind, and to attune themselves to the higher frequencies of the universe.

He guided them in the practice of meditation and mindfulness, leading them on a journey inward to discover the true nature of their being.

And as they delved deeper into the depths of their own souls, they found themselves awakening to a reality beyond their wildest dreams.

They experienced moments of profound stillness and peace, where the chatter of the mind fell away, and they were enveloped in the embrace of the divine.

They saw visions of otherworldly beauty and heard whispers of ancient wisdom, as the veils of illusion were lifted, and the truth of existence revealed itself to them.
Solarius taught them that ascension was not a destination, but a journey, a continual unfolding of the soul towards greater levels of awareness and understanding.
He encouraged them to let go of attachment to the material world and to surrender to the divine flow, trusting in the wisdom of the universe to guide them on their path.
And as they released their fears and embraced the light of their own divinity, they felt themselves ascending to higher realms of consciousness, where love and unity reigned supreme.
They realized that they were not separate from the Cosmic Source, but one with it, connected to all things in the web of creation.
And as they basked in the radiance of divine love, they knew that they had entered into a new era of enlightenment, where the possibilities were endless, and the journey of the soul was eternal.
Blessed are those who embark on the journey of ascension, for they shall rise above the limitations of the physical world and dwell in the realms of light and love for all eternity.

Chapter 7: The Unity of All Things

Solarius gathered the people beneath the starlit sky, where the vastness of the universe stretched out before them like a tapestry woven with light. He spoke to them of the unity of all things, of the interconnectedness of every living being and the oneness of all existence.
Solarius taught them that at the deepest level of reality, there was no separation, no division between one being and another, but only a seamless web of interconnectedness that bound all things together.
He showed them how every thought, every word, and every action rippled outwards, affecting the world around them in ways they could scarcely imagine.
Solarius spoke of the law of karma, the principle of cause and effect that governed the universe, showing them that their actions had consequences, not only for themselves but for all of creation.
He urged them to tread lightly upon the earth, to live in harmony with nature, and to treat every living being with kindness and compassion.
For he knew that when they acted from a place of love and understanding, they contributed to the healing and upliftment of the entire planet.

Solarius taught them that they were not separate from the earth, but intrinsically connected to it, and that by honoring and respecting the natural world, they honored and respected themselves.
And as they opened their hearts to the beauty and wonder of creation, they felt a deep sense of reverence and awe for the miracle of life.
They saw themselves reflected in the eyes of every living creature, and felt a kinship with all beings, whether human, animal, or plant.
Solarius showed them that they were part of something greater than themselves, part of a vast and magnificent tapestry of life that stretched across the cosmos.
And as they embraced the unity of all things, they felt themselves expanding beyond the confines of their individual selves, merging with the infinite expanse of the universe.
They realized that they were not alone, but part of a grand and beautiful symphony of existence, where every note, every chord, contributed to the harmonious unfolding of creation.
And as they surrendered to the flow of life, they felt themselves carried along on the currents of divine grace, guided by the unseen hand of destiny.

Blessed are those who recognize the unity of all things, for they shall dwell in the heart of the Cosmic Source, where love and light shine eternal.

Chapter 8: The Dance of Light and Shadow

Solarius led the people to a place where the sun dipped low on the horizon, casting long shadows across the landscape.
As they gathered in the fading light, he spoke to them of the dance of light and shadow, the eternal interplay of duality that permeated the fabric of existence.
Solarius taught them that light and shadow were not opposing forces, but complementary aspects of the same divine unity, each necessary for the other to exist.
He showed them how the light illuminated the darkness, revealing the hidden beauty and potential within, while the shadow provided contrast and depth, giving form and substance to the light.
Solarius urged them not to fear the darkness, but to embrace it as an integral part of the journey of the soul, for it was only through confronting their shadows that they could truly know themselves.

He taught them that every challenge, every obstacle they faced was an opportunity for growth and transformation, a chance to shine the light of awareness into the darkest corners of their being. And as they embraced their shadows with love and acceptance, they found that the darkness held within it the seeds of their greatest gifts and strengths.

Solarius showed them that they were not defined by their shadows, but by the light that shone within them, illuminating their path and guiding their steps.

He encouraged them to shine their light brightly, even in the darkest of times, knowing that their inner radiance would dispel the shadows and illuminate the way forward.

And so they danced in the twilight, moving gracefully between the light and the shadow, embracing the full spectrum of their being with joy and reverence.

They understood that life was a delicate balance between the two, a dance of opposites that gave rise to the richness and diversity of existence. Solarius taught them that it was only by embracing both the light and the shadow that they could experience true wholeness and integration, for each contained within it the seeds of the other.

And as they danced beneath the stars, they felt themselves merging with the rhythm of the universe, surrendering to the ebb and flow of life with grace and humility.

Blessed are those who embrace the dance of light and shadow, for they shall find balance and harmony in the ever-changing symphony of existence.

And so it was that Solarius led the people into the heart of the mystery, where light and shadow danced together in perfect harmony, and the unity of all things was revealed.

Chapter 9: The Awakening of the Heart

Solarius gathered the people in a sacred grove, where the air was filled with the sweet scent of flowers and the gentle rustle of leaves.

As they sat in quiet contemplation, he spoke to them of the awakening of the heart, the journey of love that transcended all boundaries and connected them to the very essence of existence.

Solarius taught them that love was the highest vibration in the universe, the force that held the stars in their courses and the planets in their orbits.

He showed them that love was not just an emotion, but a state of being, a way of relating to the world with compassion, kindness, and understanding.

Solarius urged them to open their hearts fully, to release the walls they had built around them, and to allow the love of the Cosmic Source to flow through them unimpeded.

He taught them that love was the true nature of their souls, and that by embracing it fully, they could heal themselves and the world around them.

And as they opened their hearts to love, they felt a deep sense of connection to all of creation, a oneness that transcended time and space.

They saw themselves reflected in the eyes of every living being, and felt a kinship with all of life, from the tiniest insect to the mightiest oak.

Solarius showed them that love was the key to transformation, the alchemical catalyst that could transmute even the darkest of shadows into light.

He taught them that when they approached life with love in their hearts, miracles unfolded before them, as if by magic.

And so they embraced the teachings of Solarius with open hearts and open minds, knowing that love was the most powerful force in the universe.

They resolved to live each moment with love as their guide, knowing that in love, all things were possible.

And as they walked the path of love, they felt themselves growing lighter and brighter, as if their very souls were expanding to encompass the infinite expanse of the cosmos.

Blessed are those who awaken to the power of love, for they shall know true joy and fulfillment in every moment of their lives.

And so it was that Solarius led the people into the heart of love, where they discovered the true essence of their being, and found themselves bathed in the radiant light of divine love for all eternity.

Chapter 10: The Path of Inner Peace

Solarius led the people to the shores of a tranquil lake, where the waters shimmered in the light of the setting sun.

As they sat in silent meditation, he spoke to them of the path of inner peace, the journey of finding stillness and serenity amidst the chaos of the world.

Solarius taught them that true peace could only be found within, in the quiet depths of their own souls, beyond the distractions and disturbances of the external world.

He showed them that peace was not the absence of conflict, but the presence of harmony, a state of being that transcended the dualities of pleasure and pain, gain and loss.

Solarius urged them to let go of attachment to outcomes, to surrender to the flow of life with acceptance and equanimity.

He taught them that peace was a choice, a conscious decision to release the burdens of the past and the anxieties of the future, and to dwell fully in the present moment.

And as they practiced the art of mindfulness and presence, they felt a deep sense of peace wash over them, like a gentle breeze caressing their souls.

They saw that the world around them was but a reflection of their inner state, and that by cultivating inner peace, they could create a ripple effect of tranquility that would spread throughout the entire cosmos.

Solarius showed them that peace was not something to be sought outside of themselves, but a treasure that lay within, waiting to be discovered and embraced.

He taught them that when they turned inward and connected with the stillness of their own being, they tapped into a wellspring of peace that was eternal and unshakable.

And so they embarked on the path of inner peace, letting go of the need to control and manipulate their circumstances, and trusting in the wisdom of the universe to guide them on their journey.

They found that as they surrendered to the flow of life, they were carried along on the currents of divine grace, and that every challenge became an opportunity for growth and transformation.

And as they walked the path of inner peace, they felt themselves becoming lighter and freer, as if the weight of the world had been lifted from their shoulders.

Blessed are those who walk the path of inner peace, for they shall dwell in the kingdom of heaven here on earth, and know the true joy of being alive.

And so it was that Solarius led the people into the heart of peace, where they found solace and sanctuary in the embrace of their own divine essence, and knew that they were home.

Chapter 11: The Wisdom of Surrender

Solarius gathered the people beneath the canopy of the ancient trees, where the leaves whispered secrets of ages past and the earth pulsed with the rhythm of life.

As they sat in reverent silence, he spoke to them of the wisdom of surrender, the transformative power of letting go and allowing the divine flow of the universe to guide their path.

Solarius taught them that surrender was not a sign of weakness, but a profound act of trust and faith in the wisdom of the Cosmic Source.

He showed them that when they released their grip on control and surrendered to the unfolding of life, they opened themselves to infinite possibilities and blessings beyond their wildest dreams.

Solarius urged them to surrender not only their desires and expectations, but also their fears and doubts, knowing that they were held in the loving embrace of the universe.

He taught them that surrender was an act of humility, a recognition of their own limitations and a willingness to surrender to a higher power.

And as they surrendered to the flow of life, they felt a deep sense of peace and liberation wash over them, as if the weight of the world had been lifted from their shoulders.

They saw that in surrendering to the divine will, they were not giving up their power, but aligning themselves with the greater wisdom of the universe.

Solarius showed them that when they surrendered to the present moment, they stepped into the realm of infinite possibility, where miracles awaited them at every turn.

And so they embraced the wisdom of surrender with open hearts and open minds, knowing that in letting go, they were opening themselves to the fullness of life.

They surrendered to the flow of life, trusting that the universe would always provide for their highest good, even in the face of uncertainty and challenge.

And as they surrendered to the divine flow, they felt themselves carried along on the currents of grace, guided by the unseen hand of destiny.

Blessed are those who surrender to the wisdom of the universe, for they shall find peace and fulfillment in every moment of their lives.

And so it was that Solarius led the people into the heart of surrender, where they discovered the true freedom that comes from letting go and allowing the divine will to unfold.

Chapter 12: The Power of Forgiveness

Solarius gathered the people in a sacred circle, where the fire danced and the stars shimmered in the velvet sky.

As they sat in the glow of the flames, he spoke to them of the power of forgiveness, the transformative force that could heal even the deepest wounds of the soul.

Solarius taught them that forgiveness was not about condoning or excusing the actions of others, but about releasing the burden of anger and resentment that weighed heavy on their hearts.

He showed them that holding onto grudges and grievances only served to keep them bound to the past, preventing them from fully embracing the present moment and moving forward with grace and ease.

Solarius urged them to let go of the chains of unforgiveness that shackled them to pain and suffering, and to open their hearts to the healing power of love and compassion.

He taught them that forgiveness was an act of self-love, a gift they gave to themselves as much as to others, freeing them from the prison of their own resentment and bitterness.

And as they embraced the practice of forgiveness, they felt a weight lift from their shoulders, as if a great burden had been lifted from their souls.

They saw that forgiveness was not a sign of weakness, but of strength, a courageous act of liberation that set them free from the chains of the past.

Solarius showed them that when they forgave others, they also forgave themselves, releasing the shame and guilt that had held them captive for so long.

And so they opened their hearts to forgiveness, letting go of old hurts and grievances, and embracing the healing power of love and compassion.

They saw that forgiveness was a journey, a process of letting go and allowing the light of healing to enter their hearts and illuminate their souls.

And as they forgave, they felt a sense of peace and freedom wash over them, as if the wounds of the past had been transformed into sources of strength and wisdom.

Blessed are those who forgive, for they shall know true liberation and peace.

And so it was that Solarius led the people into the heart of forgiveness, where they discovered the transformative power of love and compassion, and found healing for their wounded souls.

Chapter 13: The Divine Within

Solarius took the people to a mountaintop, where they could feel the crisp air and see the vast expanse of the world below.

As they gazed out at the horizon, he spoke to them of the divine spark that dwelled within each and every one of them, a radiant light that connected them to the Cosmic Source.

Solarius taught them that they were not separate from the divine, but intrinsically connected to it, woven into the very fabric of creation.

He showed them that the divine spark within them was a source of infinite power and potential, waiting to be awakened and unleashed.

Solarius urged them to look within, to connect with the divine presence that dwelled in the depths of their own souls, and to recognize their own divinity.

He taught them that they were not mere mortals, but divine beings of light, capable of manifesting miracles and creating worlds with the power of their thoughts and intentions.

And as they connected with the divine within, they felt a sense of empowerment and purpose wash over them, as if they had tapped into an infinite reservoir of strength and wisdom.

They saw that the answers they sought were not to be found outside of themselves, but within, in the sacred temple of their own hearts.

Solarius showed them that when they aligned themselves with the divine presence within, they could overcome any obstacle and transcend any limitation.

And so they embraced their divine nature with open hearts and open minds, knowing that they were co-creators with the Cosmic Source, and that the power to shape their destiny lay within them.

They saw that the divine spark within them was a beacon of light in the darkness, guiding them on their journey and illuminating the path ahead.

And as they embraced their divinity, they felt themselves expanding beyond the confines of their physical bodies, merging with the infinite expanse of the cosmos.

Blessed are those who recognize the divine within, for they shall know the true nature of their being and walk the path of enlightenment.

And so it was that Solarius led the people into the heart of their own divinity, where they discovered the infinite power and potential that lay within them, and realized that they were truly divine beings of light.

Chapter 14: The Radiance of Gratitude

Solarius gathered the people beneath the canopy of a star-studded sky, where the moon cast its gentle glow upon the earth.

As they stood in awe of the celestial display above them, he spoke to them of the power of gratitude, the transformative energy that could illuminate even the darkest of nights.

Solarius taught them that gratitude was more than just a fleeting emotion or polite gesture, but a profound way of relating to the world with reverence and appreciation.

He showed them that when they cultivated an attitude of gratitude, they opened themselves to the abundant blessings that surrounded them, and invited more blessings into their lives.

Solarius urged them to count their blessings, not just in times of abundance, but also in times of hardship and struggle, for even in the darkest of moments, there was always something to be thankful for.

He taught them that gratitude was a choice, a conscious decision to focus on the positive aspects of life and to celebrate the beauty and wonder of existence.

And as they embraced the practice of gratitude, they felt a shift occur within them, as if a veil had been lifted from their eyes, revealing the magic and miracles that surrounded them at every turn.

They saw that gratitude was a magnet for abundance, drawing to them blessings and opportunities that they had never imagined possible.

Solarius showed them that when they lived with an open heart and a spirit of gratitude, they became co-creators with the universe, manifesting their dreams and desires with ease and grace.

And so they began to give thanks for the simple joys of life – the warmth of the sun on their faces, the laughter of children, the beauty of a flower in bloom.

They gave thanks for the challenges that had made them stronger, the setbacks that had taught them valuable lessons, and the moments of grace that had filled their hearts with joy.

And as they expressed their gratitude, they felt a sense of abundance and fulfillment wash over them, as if the universe itself were smiling down upon them in approval.

Blessed are those who cultivate an attitude of gratitude, for they shall know the true richness and abundance of life.

And so it was that Solarius led the people into the heart of gratitude, where they discovered the radiant power of thanksgiving, and realized that gratitude was the key that unlocked the door to a life filled with blessings and abundance.

Chapter 15: The Dance of Creation

Solarius led the people to a clearing in the forest, where the earth was carpeted with a tapestry of wildflowers, and the air was alive with the hum of bees and the song of birds.

As they stood amidst the beauty of nature, he spoke to them of the dance of creation, the sacred rhythm that pulsed through the heart of all existence.

Solarius taught them that creation was not a static event, but an ongoing process, a perpetual dance of energy and consciousness that unfolded in every moment.

He showed them that they were not mere spectators, but active participants in the dance of creation, co-creators with the Cosmic Source, shaping their reality with every thought, word, and action.

Solarius urged them to dance with life, to surrender to the divine flow and allow their inner wisdom to guide their steps.

He taught them that when they aligned themselves with the rhythm of creation, they tapped into a wellspring of creativity and inspiration that flowed from the very heart of the universe.

And as they danced with abandon, they felt themselves merging with the energy of creation, becoming one with the pulsating heartbeat of the cosmos.

They saw that creation was not a linear process, but a multidimensional symphony of light and sound, color and texture, weaving together to form the rich tapestry of existence.

Solarius showed them that they were not bound by the limitations of time and space, but free to explore the vast expanse of the cosmos with their minds and imaginations.

And so they danced with joy and exuberance, celebrating the beauty and wonder of creation, and reveling in the infinite possibilities that lay before them.

They danced with the trees and the flowers, the stars and the planets, feeling themselves connected to all of life in a cosmic celebration of unity and harmony.

And as they surrendered to the dance of creation, they felt a sense of liberation and empowerment wash over them, as if they had tapped into a source of infinite creativity and potential.

Blessed are those who dance with creation, for they shall know the true joy and beauty of existence.

And so it was that Solarius led the people into the heart of the dance of creation, where they discovered the infinite power and majesty of the Cosmic Source, and realized that they were the architects of their own destiny.

Chapter 16: The Harmony of Balance

Solarius guided the people to a serene garden, where the gentle breeze whispered through the leaves and the fragrance of blossoms filled the air. As they walked amidst the beauty of nature, he spoke to them of the harmony of balance, the delicate equilibrium that permeated the universe. Solarius taught them that balance was not a static state, but a dynamic interplay of opposites, a dance of light and dark, yin and yang, that gave rise to the richness and diversity of life.

He showed them that when they embraced the principles of balance in their lives, they experienced a sense of peace and fulfillment that transcended all understanding.

Solarius urged them to seek balance in all things – in their thoughts and emotions, in their relationships and endeavors, knowing that true harmony could only be found when all aspects of their being were in alignment.

He taught them that balance was not about achieving perfection or eliminating all challenges, but about finding the middle way, the path of moderation and temperance that led to inner peace and tranquility.

And as they embraced the practice of balance, they felt a sense of wholeness and integration wash over them, as if they had come home to themselves.

They saw that balance was not a destination, but a journey, a continual process of adjustment and refinement that required mindfulness and awareness.

Solarius showed them that when they lived in harmony with the rhythms of nature and the cycles of the cosmos, they tapped into a source of wisdom and guidance that flowed from the very heart of the universe.

And so they sought balance in their lives, cultivating a sense of equilibrium and stability that allowed them to navigate the ups and downs of existence with grace and ease.

They balanced their work and rest, their giving and receiving, their action and contemplation, knowing that in the dance of life, it was the harmony of

balance that held the key to true happiness and fulfillment.
And as they walked the path of balance, they felt themselves becoming more centered and grounded, as if they were rooted deeply in the earth and reaching for the stars.
Blessed are those who seek balance in all things, for they shall know the peace that surpasses all understanding.
And so it was that Solarius led the people into the heart of balance, where they discovered the timeless wisdom of the cosmic dance, and found themselves dancing in perfect harmony with the rhythms of the universe.

Chapter 17: The Gateway of Transformation

Solarius guided the people to the edge of a deep forest, where ancient trees stood tall and majestic, their branches reaching toward the heavens.
As they entered the sacred grove, he spoke to them of the gateway of transformation, the threshold between the old and the new, the known and the unknown.
Solarius taught them that transformation was a natural and inevitable part of life, a process of

growth and evolution that unfolded in every moment.

He showed them that just as the caterpillar transforms into a butterfly, so too were they capable of undergoing profound and miraculous transformations in their own lives.

Solarius urged them to embrace change with courage and grace, knowing that it was through the process of transformation that they could shed their old selves and emerge into the fullness of their being.

He taught them that transformation was not always easy or comfortable, but that it was always necessary for their growth and evolution as spiritual beings.

And as they stood at the threshold of transformation, they felt a sense of excitement and anticipation wash over them, as if they were on the brink of a great adventure.

They saw that transformation was not a destination, but a journey, a continual unfolding of their potential and possibilities.

Solarius showed them that when they embraced the process of transformation with an open heart and mind, they could tap into a wellspring of creativity and inspiration that would propel them forward on their path.

And so they stepped boldly into the gateway of transformation, letting go of the past and embracing the unknown future with faith and trust.

They felt themselves shedding old patterns and beliefs, releasing what no longer served them, and stepping into the fullness of their power and potential.

And as they journeyed through the gateway of transformation, they felt a sense of liberation and renewal wash over them, as if they had been reborn into a higher state of consciousness.

Blessed are those who embrace the process of transformation, for they shall know the true freedom and joy of becoming.

And so it was that Solarius led the people through the gateway of transformation, where they discovered the power and potential that lay dormant within them, and realized that they were capable of creating a life of beauty and wonder beyond their wildest dreams.

Chapter 18: The Light Within

Solarius led the people to a sacred temple, where the walls were adorned with images of celestial beings and the air was filled with the fragrance of incense.

As they entered the hallowed halls, he spoke to them of the light within, the divine spark that dwelled at the core of their being, radiating with the brilliance of a thousand suns.

Solarius taught them that they were not just physical beings, but beings of light and spirit, incarnations of the Cosmic Source itself.

He showed them that the light within them was eternal and unchanging, a beacon of hope and inspiration that could never be extinguished.

Solarius urged them to connect with the light within, to nurture and cultivate it, knowing that it was the source of their strength and power.

He taught them that when they aligned themselves with the light within, they tapped into a reservoir of wisdom and guidance that flowed from the very heart of the universe.

And as they connected with their inner light, they felt a sense of peace and clarity wash over them, as if they had come home to themselves. They saw that the light within them was a reflection of the divine light that permeated all of creation, connecting them to the very essence of existence.

Solarius showed them that when they embraced their inner light, they became beacons of love and compassion, shining their light into the darkest corners of the world and illuminating the path for others to follow.

And so they embraced their inner light with open hearts and open minds, knowing that it was the key to their liberation and enlightenment.

They nurtured their inner light with love and care, allowing it to shine brightly and guide them on their journey through life.

And as they basked in the radiance of their own inner light, they felt themselves expanding beyond the limitations of their physical bodies, merging with the infinite expanse of the cosmos.

Blessed are those who connect with the light within, for they shall know the true beauty and majesty of their own divine essence.

And so it was that Solarius led the people into the heart of their own inner light, where they discovered the infinite power and wisdom that lay within them, and realized that they were truly beings of light and spirit, shining with the brilliance of the stars themselves.

Chapter 19: The Unity of All Creation

Solarius led the people to a sacred grove, where the trees stood tall and proud, their branches reaching out to embrace the sky.

As they gathered in the shade of the ancient trees, he spoke to them of the unity of all creation, the interconnectedness that bound all beings together in a tapestry of life.

Solarius taught them that they were not separate from the world around them, but intimately connected to every living thing, from the tiniest blade of grass to the mightiest mountain.

He showed them that the same divine essence that flowed through them also flowed through every creature and every aspect of nature, connecting them in a web of love and light.

Solarius urged them to see themselves not as isolated individuals, but as integral parts of a greater whole, each one a unique expression of the Cosmic Source.

He taught them that when they embraced the unity of all creation, they opened themselves to a deeper understanding of themselves and the world around them.

And as they opened their hearts to the interconnectedness of all life, they felt a sense of reverence and awe wash over them, as if they were standing in the presence of the divine itself.

They saw that every tree, every bird, every flower was a manifestation of the same divine energy that dwelled within them, each one a reflection of the infinite beauty and wisdom of the universe.

Solarius showed them that when they honored and respected all beings as sacred, they contributed to the harmonious balance of the cosmos, fostering peace and goodwill wherever they went.

And so they embraced the unity of all creation with open hearts and open minds, knowing that in the interconnectedness of all life lay the key to true happiness and fulfillment.

They saw themselves mirrored in the eyes of every living being, and felt a deep sense of kinship and compassion for all of creation.

And as they walked the path of unity, they felt themselves expanding beyond the limitations of their individual selves, merging with the infinite expanse of the cosmos.

Blessed are those who recognize the unity of all creation, for they shall know the true beauty and majesty of the universe.

And so it was that Solarius led the people into the heart of unity, where they discovered the interconnectedness of all life, and realized that they were but threads in the tapestry of creation, woven together in a symphony of love and light.

Chapter 20: The Ripple of Compassion

Solarius took the people to the banks of a tranquil river, where the water flowed gently, carrying with it the reflections of the world around. As they sat beside the river, he spoke to them of the ripple of compassion, the gentle wave of kindness that spread outward from the heart and touched the lives of all beings.

Solarius taught them that compassion was more than just a feeling or emotion, but a way of being in the world, a practice of empathy and understanding that transcended all boundaries.

He showed them that when they opened their hearts to compassion, they became vessels of love and healing, bringing comfort and solace to those in need.

Solarius urged them to cultivate compassion in their daily lives, to see the world through the eyes of love and to treat all beings with kindness and respect.

He taught them that compassion was a powerful force for positive change, capable of transforming hearts and minds, and creating a world of peace and harmony.

And as they embraced the practice of compassion, they felt a sense of connection and unity with all beings, as if they were part of a vast tapestry of love that stretched across the cosmos.

They saw that every act of compassion, no matter how small, sent out ripples of love and healing that reverberated throughout the universe, touching the lives of countless beings.

Solarius showed them that when they extended compassion to others, they also extended it to themselves, for they were all interconnected, bound together by the same divine thread of love. And so they opened their hearts to compassion, allowing it to flow freely and unconditionally, knowing that in the giving and receiving of compassion, they were participating in the divine dance of creation.

They saw the beauty in every being, and felt a deep sense of gratitude for the opportunity to share their love and compassion with the world. And as they walked the path of compassion, they felt themselves becoming more aligned with the higher frequencies of love and light, and their hearts expanded with joy and fulfillment.

Blessed are those who cultivate compassion in their hearts, for they shall know the true beauty and majesty of the human spirit.

And so it was that Solarius led the people into the heart of compassion, where they discovered the transformative power of love, and realized that in the practice of compassion, they could create a world of peace and harmony for all beings.

Chapter 21: The Eternal Now

Solarius brought the people to a serene meadow, where the wildflowers danced in the breeze and the sun cast its golden glow upon the earth.

As they sat in the warmth of the sun, he spoke to them of the eternal now, the timeless moment that exists beyond the confines of past and future.

Solarius taught them that the present moment was the gateway to eternity, a sacred space where they could experience the fullness of life in all its beauty and wonder.

He showed them that when they let go of regrets and worries about the past, and fears and anxieties about the future, they could fully immerse themselves in the richness of the present moment.

Solarius urged them to awaken to the magic of the present moment, to be fully present and aware of the miracles unfolding all around them.

He taught them that in the eternal now, there was no judgment or expectation, only acceptance and appreciation for the beauty of life as it is.

And as they surrendered to the flow of the present moment, they felt a sense of peace and contentment wash over them, as if they had come home to themselves.

They saw that in the eternal now, there was no separation between themselves and the world around them, but a deep sense of oneness and interconnectedness with all of creation.

Solarius showed them that when they lived in the present moment, they tapped into a wellspring of joy and vitality that flowed from the very heart of the universe.

And so they embraced the eternal now with open hearts and open minds, knowing that it was in this moment, and this moment alone, that they could truly experience the fullness of life.

They let go of the need to control or manipulate the future, and instead surrendered to the divine flow of the present moment, trusting that all was unfolding exactly as it should.

And as they lived each moment with mindfulness and presence, they felt themselves becoming more aligned with the rhythms of the universe, and their hearts filled with gratitude for the gift of life.

Blessed are those who dwell in the eternal now, for they shall know the true joy and beauty of existence.

And so it was that Solarius led the people into the heart of the eternal now, where they discovered the timeless essence of their being, and realized that in the present moment, they were free to live fully and authentically, in harmony with the flow of life.

Chapter 22: The Awakening of Consciousness

Solarius gathered the people beneath the starry sky, where the constellations twinkled with ancient wisdom and the moon bathed the earth in its gentle light.
As they gazed up at the celestial spectacle above, he spoke to them of the awakening of consciousness, the expansion of awareness that leads to enlightenment.
Solarius taught them that consciousness was more than just the sum of their thoughts and perceptions, but the very essence of their being, the eternal spark of divine intelligence that animated their existence.
He showed them that when they transcended the limitations of the ego mind and opened themselves to the infinite possibilities of the cosmos, they could tap into a source of wisdom and guidance that flowed from the very heart of the universe.
Solarius urged them to awaken from the slumber of unconsciousness, to become active participants

in the unfolding of their own evolution, and to embrace the fullness of their potential as conscious co-creators with the Cosmic Source.

He taught them that the awakening of consciousness was a journey of self-discovery and self-realization, a process of remembering who they truly were and reclaiming their birthright as divine beings of light.

And as they opened their hearts and minds to the higher frequencies of consciousness, they felt a sense of expansion and liberation wash over them, as if they had stepped out of the shadows and into the light of truth.

They saw that consciousness was not confined to the boundaries of their physical bodies, but extended beyond the limits of time and space, connecting them to the infinite expanse of the cosmos.

Solarius showed them that when they aligned themselves with the higher dimensions of consciousness, they could access a deeper understanding of themselves and the world around them, and navigate their lives with clarity and purpose.

And so they embarked on the journey of awakening, diving deep into the depths of their own souls, and unlocking the hidden treasures of wisdom and insight that lay within.

They embraced the challenges and struggles that arose along the way, knowing that each obstacle was an opportunity for growth and transformation. And as they expanded their consciousness and embraced the fullness of their being, they felt themselves becoming more aligned with the divine flow of the universe, and their hearts filled with love and gratitude for the miracle of existence.

Blessed are those who awaken to the fullness of their consciousness, for they shall know the true beauty and majesty of the cosmos.

And so it was that Solarius led the people on the journey of awakening, where they discovered the infinite depths of their own consciousness, and realized that in the expansion of their awareness, they were opening themselves to the boundless possibilities of the universe.

Chapter 23: The Wisdom of Surrender

Solarius led the people to a tranquil oasis, where the waters shimmered in the sunlight and the palm trees swayed gently in the breeze. As they sat beside the peaceful waters, he spoke to them of the wisdom of surrender, the art of letting go and allowing the natural flow of life to unfold.

Solarius taught them that surrender was not a sign of weakness, but a powerful act of trust and faith in the wisdom of the universe.

He showed them that when they surrendered to the divine flow of life, they released resistance and opened themselves to the infinite possibilities that lay before them.

Solarius urged them to surrender their fears and doubts, their desires and attachments, knowing that in the surrendering, they found true freedom and liberation.

He taught them that surrender was not about giving up or relinquishing control, but about aligning themselves with the higher intelligence of the cosmos and allowing their lives to be guided by the wisdom of the universe.

And as they surrendered to the divine flow, they felt a sense of peace and serenity wash over them, as if they were being cradled in the arms of the divine mother.

They saw that in the surrendering, they let go of the need to struggle and strive, and instead surrendered to the effortless flow of grace that carried them forward on their journey.

Solarius showed them that when they surrendered to the present moment, they tapped into a source of power and wisdom that flowed from the very heart of the universe.

And so they surrendered to the divine flow with open hearts and open minds, knowing that in the letting go, they found true peace and fulfillment. They released their grip on the illusions of control and certainty, and embraced the uncertainty and mystery of life with joy and gratitude.

And as they surrendered to the divine flow, they felt themselves becoming more aligned with the rhythms of the cosmos, and their hearts filled with love and compassion for all of creation.

Blessed are those who surrender to the wisdom of the universe, for they shall know the true beauty and majesty of existence.

And so it was that Solarius led the people into the wisdom of surrender, where they discovered the power and liberation that came from letting go, and realized that in the surrendering, they found true peace and serenity in the arms of the divine.

Chapter 24: The Dance of Life

Solarius gathered the people beneath the open sky, where the stars sparkled like diamonds and the moon cast its silvery glow upon the earth. As they stood amidst the beauty of the night, he spoke to them of the dance of life, the eternal rhythm that pulsed through the cosmos and animated all of creation.

Solarius taught them that life was not a solitary journey, but a grand dance of interconnectedness and unity, where each being played a vital role in the unfolding tapestry of existence.

He showed them that just as the planets revolved around the sun in a celestial dance, so too did they move in harmony with the rhythms of the universe, each step a part of the cosmic choreography.

Solarius urged them to embrace the dance of life with joy and enthusiasm, to surrender to the music of the universe and allow their hearts to guide their steps.

He taught them that in the dance of life, there were no mistakes or missteps, only opportunities for growth and expansion.

And as they surrendered to the flow of the dance, they felt a sense of liberation and empowerment wash over them, as if they had tapped into a source of infinite creativity and vitality.

They saw that in the dance of life, they were not separate from the world around them, but intimately connected to every living thing, sharing in the joy and sorrow, the laughter and tears of all beings.

Solarius showed them that when they danced with abandon, they tapped into a wellspring of joy and

inspiration that flowed from the very heart of the universe.
And so they danced beneath the stars, letting go of their inhibitions and allowing the music of the cosmos to carry them away.
They felt themselves merging with the rhythm of the universe, becoming one with the pulsating heartbeat of creation.
And as they danced, they felt a sense of oneness and unity with all of existence, as if they were part of a cosmic symphony that reverberated throughout the cosmos.
Blessed are those who dance the dance of life, for they shall know the true joy and beauty of existence.
And so it was that Solarius led the people into the dance of life, where they discovered the infinite grace and beauty that lay within them, and realized that in the surrendering to the rhythm of the universe, they found true freedom and liberation in the eternal dance of creation.

Chapter 25: The Harmony of Diversity

Solarius guided the people to a bustling marketplace, where vendors from far and wide gathered to sell their wares, and the air was filled with the sounds of different languages and dialects.

As they walked through the vibrant marketplace, he spoke to them of the harmony of diversity, the beauty that arises when individuals from all walks of life come together in unity and respect.

Solarius taught them that diversity was not a source of division, but a reflection of the rich tapestry of human experience, a celebration of the myriad expressions of the divine.

He showed them that just as each flower in a garden adds to the overall beauty of the landscape, so too did each individual bring their own unique gifts and talents to the world.

Solarius urged them to embrace diversity with open hearts and open minds, to see the beauty in differences and to celebrate the richness that comes from living in a world of infinite variety.

He taught them that when they honored and respected the uniqueness of each individual, they contributed to the harmonious balance of the cosmos, fostering peace and goodwill wherever they went.

And as they embraced diversity with love and acceptance, they felt a sense of unity and connection wash over them, as if they were all threads in the same cosmic tapestry.

They saw that in the diversity of the world, there was strength and resilience, a resilience that came from the ability to adapt and evolve in the face of change.

Solarius showed them that when they recognized the inherent value and worth of each individual, they contributed to the creation of a world where all beings were honored and respected.

And so they embraced diversity with open hearts and open minds, knowing that in the celebration of differences, they found true beauty and harmony.

They saw themselves reflected in the eyes of every person they met, and felt a deep sense of kinship and compassion for all of humanity.

And as they walked the path of unity amidst diversity, they felt themselves becoming more aligned with the higher frequencies of love and light, and their hearts expanded with joy and fulfillment.

Blessed are those who embrace diversity with love and acceptance, for they shall know the true beauty and majesty of the human spirit.

And so it was that Solarius led the people into the harmony of diversity, where they discovered the beauty and richness that comes from living in a world of infinite variety, and realized that in the celebration of differences, they found true unity and oneness with all of creation.

Chapter 26: The Power of Gratitude

    Solarius guided the people to a tranquil garden, where the scent of blooming flowers filled the air and the gentle rustle of leaves provided a soothing melody.

As they walked through the garden, he spoke to them of the power of gratitude, the transformative force that can shift one's perspective and bring abundance into their lives.

Solarius taught them that gratitude was more than just saying "thank you," but a deep appreciation for the blessings that surrounded them, both big and small.

He showed them that when they cultivated an attitude of gratitude, they opened themselves to the flow of abundance and prosperity that permeated the universe.

Solarius urged them to embrace gratitude as a way of life, to see every experience as an opportunity for growth and learning, and to find something to be grateful for in every moment.

He taught them that when they focused their attention on what they had rather than what they lacked, they shifted their energy from scarcity to abundance, and attracted more blessings into their lives.

And as they embraced the practice of gratitude, they felt a sense of joy and contentment wash over them, as if they were being showered with blessings from the heavens.

They saw that in every challenge and obstacle, there was an opportunity for gratitude, a chance to learn and grow, and to become stronger and more resilient.

Solarius showed them that when they expressed gratitude for the blessings in their lives, they created a ripple effect of positivity and abundance that spread outward, touching the lives of all those around them.

And so they embraced gratitude with open hearts and open minds, knowing that in the practice of gratitude, they found true happiness and fulfillment.

They saw the beauty in every moment, and felt a deep sense of appreciation for the miracle of existence.

And as they walked the path of gratitude, they felt themselves becoming more aligned with the higher frequencies of love and light, and their hearts expanded with joy and abundance.

Blessed are those who cultivate gratitude in their hearts, for they shall know the true richness and beauty of life.

And so it was that Solarius led the people into the power of gratitude, where they discovered the transformative force that comes from acknowledging and appreciating the blessings in their lives, and realized that in the practice of gratitude, they found true abundance and prosperity in every moment.

Chapter 27: The Path of Forgiveness

Solarius guided the people to a serene mountaintop, where they could see the world spread out before them, bathed in the warm glow of the setting sun.

As they stood amidst the beauty of nature, he spoke to them of the path of forgiveness, the sacred journey of releasing the burdens of the past and embracing the freedom of the present.

Solarius taught them that forgiveness was not about condoning the actions of others or forgetting past hurts, but about releasing the hold that resentment and anger had on their hearts.

He showed them that holding onto grudges and grievances only served to imprison them in a cycle of suffering, preventing them from experiencing true peace and happiness.

Solarius urged them to embrace forgiveness as a path to healing and liberation, to let go of the past and open themselves to the possibilities of the future.

He taught them that forgiveness was a gift they gave to themselves, a way of reclaiming their power and reclaiming their peace of mind.

And as they opened their hearts to forgiveness, they felt a weight lift from their shoulders, as if they had been carrying a heavy burden for far too long.

They saw that in the act of forgiveness, they were not condoning the actions of others, but releasing themselves from the chains of resentment and bitterness that had bound them.

Solarius showed them that when they forgave others, they also forgave themselves, for they were all interconnected and bound together by the same divine thread of love.

And so they embraced the path of forgiveness with open hearts and open minds, knowing that in the letting go of the past, they found true freedom and liberation.

They saw the beauty in every being, and felt a deep sense of compassion and empathy for all of humanity.

And as they walked the path of forgiveness, they felt themselves becoming more aligned with the higher frequencies of love and light, and their hearts expanded with joy and compassion.
Blessed are those who embrace the path of forgiveness, for they shall know the true peace and liberation that comes from releasing the past.
And so it was that Solarius led the people into the sacred journey of forgiveness, where they discovered the healing power of letting go and embracing the present moment, and realized that in the act of forgiveness, they found true freedom and peace in their hearts.

Chapter 28: The Eternal Light Within

Solarius brought the people to a quiet temple, where the soft glow of candles illuminated the sacred space, casting dancing shadows on the walls.
As they entered the temple, he spoke to them of the eternal light within, the divine spark that dwelled at the core of their being, radiating love and wisdom for all eternity.
Solarius taught them that they were not mere mortals, but divine beings of light, each one a

manifestation of the Cosmic Source, shining brightly in the tapestry of creation.
He showed them that the light within them was unquenchable, a beacon of hope and guidance that could illuminate even the darkest corners of their lives.
Solarius urged them to connect with the eternal light within, to embrace their true essence as divine beings, and to allow their inner radiance to shine forth for all the world to see.
He taught them that when they aligned themselves with the light within, they tapped into a wellspring of strength and courage that flowed from the very heart of the universe.
And as they connected with their inner light, they felt a sense of peace and serenity wash over them, as if they had come home to themselves at last.
They saw that in the light within them, there was infinite potential and possibility, a creative force that could bring about positive change and transformation in their lives and in the world around them.
Solarius showed them that when they embraced their true essence as divine beings of light, they became co-creators with the Cosmic Source, manifesting their highest dreams and aspirations with ease and grace.

And so they embraced the eternal light within with open hearts and open minds, knowing that in the illumination of their inner radiance, they found true peace and fulfillment.

They saw themselves reflected in the eyes of every being they encountered, and felt a deep sense of love and compassion for all of creation.

And as they walked the path of light, they felt themselves becoming more aligned with the higher frequencies of love and wisdom, and their hearts expanded with joy and gratitude.

Blessed are those who connect with the eternal light within, for they shall know the true beauty and majesty of their divine essence.

And so it was that Solarius led the people into the temple of their own hearts, where they discovered the eternal light that dwelled within them, and realized that in the illumination of their inner radiance, they found true peace, love, and fulfillment for all eternity.

Made in the USA
Middletown, DE
30 March 2024

52136860R00035